I'm Speaking

I'm Speaking

SELECTED POEMS

RAFAEL GUILLÉN

Translated from the Spanish
by Sandy McKinney with the author

A BILINGUAL EDITION

Northwestern University Press
Evanston, Illinois

Hydra Books
Northwestern University Press
Evanston, Illinois 60208-4210

Printed in the United States of America

10 9 8 7 6 5 4 3 2 1

ISBN 0-8101-1851-3

Library of Congress Cataloging-in-Publication Data

Guillén, Rafael, 1933–
    I'm speaking : selected poems / Rafael Guillén ; translated from the
Spanish by Sandy McKinney (with the author).—Bilingual ed.
        p. cm.
    ISBN 0-8101-1851-3 (cloth : alk. paper)
    1. Guillén, Rafael, 1933– —Translations into English. I. McKinney,
Sandy. II. Title.
    PQ6613.U53 A25 2001
    861'.64—dc21   2001001418

The paper used in this publication meets the minimum requirements of the American
National Standard for Information Sciences—Permanence of Paper for Printed Library
Materials, ANSI Z39.48-1984.

Some of these translations have appeared previously in the following periodicals: *Pequod*
("The Last Gesture," "Not Fear"); *Seneca Review* ("A Friend Comes Back," "Roadshow," "To
Be an Instant," "Today Paris Doesn't Exist"); *Tendril* ("The Final Tenderness," "One Day,
with the Dawn"); and *TriQuarterly* ("The Front Room," "Mold," "Task Work").

Contents

Translator's Introduction:
A Conversation
with Rafael Guillén

*I*n 1979, while visiting in Granada, quite by chance I came upon
Moheda, at that time the most recent collection of Guillén's work. I
discovered that he was well known in Granada but not much elsewhere,
beyond the literary community of Andalusia. No one I knew in the
United States had ever heard of him. I returned to the bookstore where
I bought *Moheda*, asking for copies of his previous works, and was
informed that they were out of print but I could meet Guillén himself if
I wanted to walk around the corner to the Banco Hispano-Americano.
He met me with great cordiality and invited me to his studio, where he
presented me with one of his own copies of the anthology that included
significant poems from four of his previous books. He also agreed to give
me every possible support in the task of translating his work, for which
I had secured formal permission, into American English.

After having read everything available, and amazed by the extensive
range of theme, language, and the daring imagery of poems like "Donde
sonó una risa" and "Desguace," I was persuaded that I had discovered a
major poet. Later, taking advantage of the rare opportunity of spending
a month working closely with him every day on the translations includ-
ed in this collection, I felt it important to record his own viewpoint
about his work, his background and influences, and his aspirations. This
is the result.

MCKINNEY: American readers in general know something, but not much, about the development of the two major trends in Spanish poetry known as the Castilian and the Andalusian. How would you outline the most important elements of the Andalusian poetic tradition?

GUILLÉN: Traditionally, Andalusian poetry is characterized by its richness of expression, in language as well as imagery. There is also in Andalusia an almost sensual delight in the beauty of particular words, in their sound as well as their significance. And, above all, a predominance of feeling over pure rationality.

MCKINNEY: What aspect of your own work do you see as an extension of this tradition, and in what ways do you see yourself departing from it?

GUILLÉN: In my own work, although not by my conscious effort, I believe the tradition continues alive. If I have explored new directions, whether in the creation or re-creation of language or syntactical forms, for example, it has been precisely by immersing myself in the Andalusian poetic tradition.

MCKINNEY: Do you feel that your work, or your way of perceiving the world, has been influenced by other poetry?

GUILLÉN: There's no doubt that my work, as the work of any writer, is based on and is a continuation—as one more step forward—on the path already traveled by all the poets who preceded me. But if I have been influenced by any of them in particular, I'm not aware of it.

MCKINNEY: You have no doubt read translations of poetry written in other languages, and you know that something will always be lost. What elements of your own work do you regard as most important to be preserved in translation?

GUILLÉN: I think it's essential that the idea of the poem be conserved as fully as possible. Every poem has an argument, a theme, and since the theme is developed around a series of images, the imagery should hold together, which would require some careful thought about word choice. Line, meter, and rhythm are more difficult to capture, of course, but I would hope a translator would take tone and quality of language into account. And I'd like to see some attention paid to the use of unusual syntax, which I employ often in my later poems, and which serves to create a particular emotional tone: a hesitation of speech or thought or, on the other hand, a breathless, uninterrupted flow of words and lines leading to a resolution not necessarily anticipated. But above all, since what I write is not merely ideas, but poetry, the translation should be more than a mere exercise in word transposition; [it] should exist as a poem in its own right, with all the graces the new language offers. On the other hand, if I were able to see a literal retranslation into Spanish, I'd like to feel that I would recognize my own voice and sensibility.

MCKINNEY: I have read a great deal of contemporary Latin American and Spanish poetry, and one aspect of much of this work—its harshness, the predominance of intellect over feeling, a kind of bitter crust—seems to exist minimally in your writing. Even in the poems that treat of war and revolution, dictatorship, famine, and oppression, there is a quality of tender grief that transcends the anger and the despair so common in the contemporary poetry of almost all nations. How have you managed to maintain such a deep emotional commitment to the process of human life and to go on reaffirming your spiritual—I wouldn't say religious— values in the face of what you must have experienced in Spain, both as a participant and as a witness?

GUILLÉN: In themes such as the ones you mention, anger and desperation are going to exist, of course. But the task of poetry is to transform those feelings in such a way that they reach the heart of the reader directly with the refined emotional quality lent them by a poetic sensibility and a poetic diction. Otherwise, one would perhaps be serving justice, or charity, or politics, but not poetry. As regards what I have had to witness and live through in Spain, it has been this commitment to poetry, as a wellspring of freedom, which has helped me to cling to the emotional fidelity you speak of.

MCKINNEY: By what means did poets and philosophers stay in contact with one another during the years of repression and censorship?

GUILLÉN: During the era of censorship and repression, communication between poets and philosophers was actually very simple, since they speak a language that dictators (who aren't known, in general, for their depth of culture) don't understand. What happens, though, is that the fruits of such contacts can't be published.

MCKINNEY: How do you explain the fact that your work, which has received such an enthusiastic reception wherever it is known, has had so little popular recognition outside Granada?

GUILLÉN: We live in a time when publicity counts, and as you know, the writers who are widely read are the ones who make appearances on radio or television, or are frequently represented in magazine or newspaper interviews. Since I rarely leave Granada, I don't involve myself in seeking publicity; fame doesn't interest me. The greatest recompense for a poet is the act itself of writing a poem. Besides, I'm very independent, and in Spain poets are known by groups, or "generations." I don't belong to any groups; I'm not interested in being classified.

MCKINNEY: Suppose your work were to receive the recognition it deserves. Would you be willing to travel to other countries to lecture or give readings?

GUILLÉN: Yes, I'd travel—but only because I like to travel (assuming that I'd be able to return to Granada soon). And I'd read my poems, but not to be famous, only because every poet wants to communicate with his fellow human beings.

MCKINNEY: What are your primary aspirations as a poet? As a man?

GUILLÉN: My aspiration as a poet is that I should be read by all the men and women in the world who share my sensibilities, and it's all the same to me if that amounts to eight or eight hundred thousand. And my aspiration as a man is to keep breathing as long as possible.

I'm Speaking

Estoy hablando

Estoy diciendo amor. Una muchacha
parte un bombón de menta con los dientes
y me da la mitad.

Estoy diciendo vida. Cien mil hombres
quedan roncos gritando
que no ha sido *penalty*.

Estoy diciendo madre. Una mujer,
cantándome una copla de otros tiempos,
me limpia las narices mientras lloro.

Estoy diciendo patria. Un hombre joven
tiene sangre en las manos entreabiertas
y dice que él no ha sido.

Estoy diciendo muerte. Alguien corre
por las calles desiertas, media noche,
en busca de un notario.

Estoy diciendo fe. Un sacerdote
se descubre y eleva a Dios la vista
mientras pasa un entierro de primera.

Estoy diciendo Dios. Todas las cosas
me miran en silencio.

I'm Speaking

I'm saying love. A little girl
cracks a peppermint between her teeth
and gives me half.

I'm saying life. A hundred thousand men
go hoarse shouting it shouldn't
have been a penalty.

I'm saying mother. A woman,
singing me a song from long ago,
wipes my nose while I scream.

I'm saying my country. A young man
cups the blood in his outstretched hands
and says he didn't start it.

I'm saying death. Someone is running
through the empty streets at midnight,
looking for a notary.

I'm saying faith. A priest
bares his head and raises his eyes to God
as a first-class funeral passes.

I'm saying God. Everything
watches me in silence.

Gesto final

Un hombre está tumbado bajo el cielo.
Se le ha apagado el tacto. Las hormigas
pueden subir el trigo por su cuello.
Esto es lo más terrible de los muertos:
que la vida los cubre y los absorbe.

Porque un hombre está muerto, y en la plaza
siguen jugando al tute los de siempre,
y se espera que grane la cosecha,
y hay barcos en los puertos, preparados
para zarpar al despuntar el alba.
Un muerto es la esperanza boca abajo.

Porque un hombre está muerto y todavía
es posible que tiene en los bolsillos
un paquete empezado de tabaco.
Y esto es lo más terrible de los muertos:
que se paran de pronto entre las cosas.

Ha muerto un hombre cuando se desdobla
y se mira su cuerpo, desde enfrente,
y se tiende la mano, y se despide.
Ha muerto un hombre, irremisiblemente,
cuando mueren los que lo recordaban.

Los muertos se resisten a estar muertos
y se defienden con su peso inerte,
y es terrible su grito cuando luchan
porque sólo se oye con los ojos.

Hay que amar a los muertos, comprenderlos.
Son como niños buenos enfadados.
Les han robado el aro y la cometa
y se han quedado tristes para siempre.

The Last Gesture

A man is stretched out underneath the sky.
His sense of touch has gone out. Ants
can climb over his neck to the stalks of wheat.
This is the most terrible thing about the dead:
That life covers them and absorbs them.

Because a man is dead, and in the plaza
the regulars are playing their usual card game.
The grain is ripe for harvesting,
and boats stand at the wharf, getting ready
to weigh anchor at dawn.
A dead man is hope facedown.

Because a man is dead and it's possible
that he may have a freshly opened
pack of smokes in his pocket.
And this is the most terrible thing about the dead:
that they stop suddenly in the midst of things.

A man has died when he unfolds himself
and stands face-to-face with his body,
holds out his hand, and bids himself good-bye.
A man has died, irremediably,
when those who remembered him die.

The dead resist being dead
and defend themselves with their inert weight,
and in that struggle their screams are terrible,
because only the eyes can hear them.

We have to love the dead, to understand them.
They're like good children in a fit of sulking.
They've lost their toys, their barrel hoops and kites,
and they'll never get over being sad, not ever.

Signos en el polvo

Como el dedo que pasa
sobre la superficie polvorienta
del mueble abandonado y deja un surco
brillante que acentúa la tristeza
de lo que ya está al margen de la vida,
de lo que sigue vivo y ya no puede
participar de nuevo, ni aun con esa
pasiva y tan sencilla
manera de estar limpio allí, dispuesto
a servir para algo; como el dedo
que traza un vago signo, ajeno a todo
significado, sólo
llevado por la inercia del impulso
gratuito y que deja
constancia así en el polvo de un inútil
acto de voluntad, así, con esa
dejadez, inconsciencia casi, siento
que alguien me pasa por la vida, alguien
que, mientras piensa en otra cosa, traza
conmigo un surco, se entretiene
en dibujar un signo incomprensible
que el tiempo borrará calladamente,
que recuperará de nuevo el polvo
aún antes de que pueda interpretarse
su cifrado sentido, si es que tuvo
sentido, si es que tuvo
razón de ser tan pasajera huella.

Tracings in the Dust

Like a finger that passes
over the dusty surface
of a discarded piece of furniture and leaves
a shiny trace that accentuates the sadness
of something fallen by the wayside of life,
that goes on with its existence but can't
participate anymore, not even with that
passive and so simple way
of being cleanly there, disposed
to serve for something; like a finger
that traces a vagrant sign, apart from
any significance, simply
carried along by the inertia
of a gratuitous impulse, leaves there
in the dust proof of a pointless
act of volition, so, leaving it there,
unconsciously almost, I feel that someone
is passing through my life, someone who,
while thinking about something else, traces
a track with me, amuses himself
by drawing an incomprehensible sign
that time will silently erase,
which will be covered over again with dust
even before I can interpret
its coded significance, that is, if it had
a significance, if it had some reason
to be such a fleeting sign.

Poema por una muchacha triste

Profesas la alegría del que paga al contado.
Te limpias tristemente los besos cuando acabas
y un azul imposible te escarcha la simiente.
Las luces de la sala y un ruido de cristales
acosan tu figura sin posibles rincones.
Un aliento cargado de indomables bostezos
coagula en tu costumbre.
Tu risa se retuerce limpiando mostradores
y hay un ritmo pastoso, de alquitrán y de menta
que te muerde las piernas con dulces latigazos.

Yo te sueño contando mariposas.
Te sueño con dos trenzas, sentada junto al pozo.

Tu cabello se arrastra por las calles oscuras;
amiga de la esquina que perfila tu sombra,
muchacha de pedazos de historia acumulados.
Los rostros se acorazan de frío y de insolencia.
Se calcula al segundo la duración del beso,
hermana del sonido de tantas cerraduras,
habitante de un mundo de escaleras gastadas.
La luna del armario no te engaña del todo.
Aún te sostiene el ancla de tu perfil desnudo.
Muchacha acorralada desde siempre
contra un fondo inmutable de sábanas usadas.

Yo te sueño estrenando blanco lino.
Te sueño en un paisaje de barcos y de niños.

No sé, muchacha triste, qué nube de que otoño
te sembró de alfileres la paz de la mirada.
No sé que mano turbia
te modeló en granito la máscara del gozo.

Poem of a Sad Girl

You put on gaiety for whoever pays the tab,
sadly wipe off the kisses when it's over,
and an impossible blue frosts the seed inside you.
    The lights of the barroom and the clink of glasses
bounce off a figure with no possible soft places.
A breath charged with indomitable yawns
coagulates in your way of being.
    Your laugh turns back on itself as you wipe down the bar
with a sticky rhythm of melted tar and mint
that prickles in your thighs like gentle nibbles.

    I imagine you counting butterflies.
I see you in pigtails, seated by the well.

    Your hair drags behind you through the dark streets,
my friend of the corner that silhouettes your shadow,
girl of little scraps of misfiled history.
    The faces are armored with cold and insolence.
You measure, to the second, the duration of the kiss,
little sister of the click of so many locks,
inhabitant of a world of rundown stairways.
    The mirror on the dresser doesn't betray you entirely.
You still have the anchor of your naked shape.
Girl penned up since now and forever
against an immutable background of used sheets.

    I imagine you laying out white linen.
I see you in a landscape of boats and babies.

    I don't know, sad girl, which autumn cloud sent down
a rain of pins on the peace of your expression.
I don't know what muddy hand
hacked that mask of lust out of granite.

Fantasmas de manzanas persiguen tus arrugas.
Risas limpias asaltan tu sueño de ceniza.
¡Qué clara y qué violenta la luz que pasa al alba
volviéndote los ojos hacia adentro!
¿En qué lago tiraste la llave del sollozo?
Muchacha sumergida, dolorosa muchacha.
Una noche redonda se te posa en el vientre.

Yo te regalaría una muñeca grande.
Pondría en tu camino campos recién arados.

The ghosts of apples haunt your furrowed spaces.
Clean laughter mocks your ashen dreams.
How clear, how violent the light of dawn
that forces you to look inside yourself!
Into what lake did you throw the key to sobs?
    Girl submerged, anguished girl,
an inflated night fills up your belly.

    I'd like to give you a great big doll.
I'd turn your road through open fields, new-plowed.

Poema para la voz de Marilyn Monroe

Tu voz.
Sólo tu tibia y sinuosa voz de leche.
Sólo un aliento gutural, silbante,
modulado entre carne, tiernamente
modulado entre almohadas
de incontenible pasmo, bordeando
las simas del gemido,
del estertor acaso.
Como un tacto de fina piel abierta.
Como un espeso y claro líquido absorbente
que envuelve tus adentros, que te sube
del sexo mismo hasta los labios,
que recorre tus dulces cavidades
antes de ser el soplo
caliente y sensorial que nos sumerge.

Tu masticada voz, que te desnuda
sutilmente, insidiosamente, como
si en derredor de tu cintura fuese
creando y disipando al mismo tiempo
mil velos transparentes de saliva.

Tu voz resuelto en quejas y mohines
que trasmina como un olor a cuerpo,
un tierno olor sedoso
que se propaga en ondas, que nos roza
tan delicadamente, que es posible
sentirlo por las manos y en las piernas.

Tu voz labial, visible,
como gustando el aire, como dando
forma a posibles moldes para besos.
Tu voz de oscura selva con riachuelos.

12

Poem for the Voice of Marilyn Monroe

Your voice.
Simply your tepid and sinuous milky voice.
Only a guttural breath, wheezing,
modulated in flesh, tenderly
modulated among pillows
of uncontrollable spasms, bordering
the depths of a moan,
almost a death rattle.
Like the touch of a fine receptive skin,
like a thick and clear absorbent liquid
that bathes your insides, that rises up
from the center of your sex to your lips,
that travels through all your sweet hollows
before becoming the puff of breath,
hot and sensual, that washes over us.

Your chewed-over voice, that strips you
subtly, insidiously, as though
all around your middle it were creating
and dissipating together a thousand
transparent veils of saliva.

Your voice resolved in moans and grimaces
that leaves a scent like a fragrance of flesh,
a tender, silky fragrance
that expands in waves, that strokes us
so delicately it's possible
to feel it with our hands and in our thighs.

Your labial voice, visible,
as if tasting the air, as if creating
puckers and pouts for kisses.
Your voice like a dark forest with tiny streams.

Clavado aquí, in mi hombría,
oigo tu voz, que late entre mis dientes,
y enmudesco la radio, y cierro el gesto.
Porque tú ya estás muerta;
porque hace largos meses que estás muerta
y aún es posible el grito enfebrecido.

Oigo tu voz carnal, y me pregunto
que pasa aquí. Si acaso es esto un nuevo
pecado, o un castigo.

Stuck here in my maleness,
I hear your voice; it beats between my teeth,
and I turn off the radio and stop the gesture.
Because you are dead now;
many long months have gone by since you died
and that feverish scream is still possible.

I hear your carnal voice, and I ask myself
what goes on here. If this is perhaps some new
kind of sin, or a castigation.

Un día, con el alba

Un día, con el alba, volvía solitario
de mis cosas de hombre. Pudo ser hace tiempo.
La claridad nacía del fondo de las calles
como la pena nace del fondo de una copa.

Siempre se vuelve solo. No sé por qué las calles
parecen tan vacías cuando el amor termina.
A través de las puertas cerradas, se sentía
vagar los esposos por la humedad del sueño.

Nunca pude entenderlo. Nos subimos a un cuerpo
como se sube un niño a la rama más alta.
De pronto, bajo el cielo, el cuerpo, que era todo,
se nos va consumiendo debajo del abrazo.

De pronto comprobamos que nos falla la tierra,
que por algún resquicio la vida se derrama.
La plenitud redonda que llegó por el tacto,
por ese mismo tacto regresa y se disipa.

Por campos y tejadas resbalaban los cinco.
Muy cerca, un jasminero debía estar despierto.
Yo volvía cansado, como vuelven los hombres
que han donado su parte para el dolor del mundo.

La desnudez de un brazo. Un cuello interminable.
Dos piernas que se alejan buscando una salida.
Una cintura firme donde apoyar las manos
como cuando se vuelca el peso en el arado.

Nunca pude entenderlo. Las miradas se enfrentan
como vueltos espejos que en si mismos acaban.
Delante de los ojos hay láminas opacas
tras las que cada amante disfraza su egoísmo.

One Day, with the Dawn

One day, with the dawn, I came back alone,
the way men do. It must have been some time ago.
Clarity was born there in the depth of the streets,
the way rue is born at the bottom of a drink.

We always come back alone. I don't know why the streets
seem so empty at the end of a night of love.
Behind the closed doors, couples could be heard
shifting in the dampness of sleep.

I've never understood it. We climb onto a body
the way a boy goes for the highest branch.
And suddenly, under heaven, the body that was everything
consumes itself away beneath our embrace.

And then and there we see how earth fails us,
how life drains out through a crack under the door.
The round plenitude that came to us with a touch
in the same touch escapes and dissipates.

In the fields, over the roofs, five o'clock was ringing.
Somewhere near, a jasmine must have been coming awake.
I came back tired, the way a man comes back
who's contributed his share to the pain of the world.

The nakedness of an arm. An expanse of throat.
Two legs flung apart, seeking a release.
A firm waist to cling to with your hands,
the way you'd lean your weight against a plow.

I've never understood it. Gazes face-to-face,
like twin mirrors reflecting only each other.
In front of the eyes, an opaque film
behind which every lover conceals his egoism.

Ella estuvo muy cerca, aquella vez, de darme
algo que con el tiempo tal vez fuera un recuerdo.
Desde aquí la contemplo, pero no tiene rostro.
No sería más triste se no hubiera existido.

Nos tiramos a un cuerpo como al mar, y aprendemos
que el amor, como el agua, no opone resistencia.
Bien poco es lo que queda después, si la ternura
no inventa sus razones para seguir viviendo.

Penetramos espacios que no nos pertenecen.
La carne, como el humo, se aleja si se toca.
Hoy ya no me pregunto la razón, y me entrego,
y acepto, y disimulo; pero sé que es chantaje.

Aquel día empezaba como todos los días;
porque todos los días empiezan y no acaban.
El alba suavizaba los últimos aleros
y la luz preparaba su primer estallido.

Siempre se vuelve solo del amor. Como entonces.
Porque el hombre limita con su piel, y los sueños
sólo cuentan, no siempre, cuando un pecho, entrevisto,
nos revela de pronto nuestra gran desventura.

She was very close, that once, to giving me something
that might have become, in time, a memento.
I look at her from here, but she has no face.
It couldn't be sadder if she'd never existed.

We throw ourselves on a body as into the sea, and learn
that love, like water, doesn't offer resistance.
Precious little is what's left afterward, if tenderness
doesn't invent its reasons to keep on living.

We thrust into places that don't belong to us.
Flesh, like smoke, moves away when it's touched.
Today I don't ask for reasons, and I give myself,
and accept, and pretend; but I know it's blackmail.

That day started like any other day
because all days start and never end.
Dawn softened the last roofedges
and the light prepared its first explosion.

We always come back alone from making love. Like then,
since a man is bound in his skin, and dreams
only count, not always, when a breast, half glimpsed,
suddenly reveals to us our great misadventure.

Apenas si recuerdo

Apenas si recuerdo tu voz, pero me dueles
en alguna parcela remota de la sangre.
Te llevo en mis abismos, enrededa en el limo,
como uno de esos cuerpos que la mar no devuelve.

Era un lugar perdido para el Sur. Una playa
sin barcas pescadoras, donde el sol se vendía.
Un litoral, ya selva de luces y de idiomas,
que desdeñó vencido su obligación de arena.

La noche de aquel día nos castigó a su antojo.
Te tenía tan cerca que era inútil mirarte.
El otoño blandía carcajadas y orquestas
y la mar se mesaba furiosa los balandros.

Tu mano equilibrada, con su calor opuesto,
la ondulante templanza del alcohol. Los jardines
me llegaban lejanos a través de tu falda.
Subía mi marea de nivel por tus pechos.

Alfombrados tentáculos por las escalinatas
atraían los pasos a las bocas del ruido.
Con luces y cortinas, más arriba del tedio,
hablaban las alcobas de los grandes hoteles.

Hay momentos oscuros en que nos vence el lastre
de tanto abatimiento. Son momentos, o siglos,
en que la carne asoma su desnudez y busca
la destrucción, bebiendo la vida de sí misma.

Yo palpaba tu abrazo por mis alrededores,
pero el amor no estaba donde estaba tu abrazo.
Yo sentía tus manos encima de mi pena,
pero la nada iba delante de tus manos.

I Hardly Remember

I hardly remember your voice, but the pain of you
floats in some remote current of my blood.
I carry you in my depths, trapped in the sludge
like one of those corpses the sea refuses to give up.

It was a spoiled remnant of the South. A beach
without fishing boats, where the sun was for sale.
A stretch of shore, now a jungle of lights and languages
that grudgingly offered, defeated, its obligation of sand.

The night of that day punished us at its whim.
I held you so close I could barely see you.
Autumn was brandishing guffaws and dance bands
and the sea tore at the pleasure boats in a frenzy.

Your hand balanced, with its steady heat,
the wavering tepidness of alcohol. The gardens
came at me from far away through your skirt.
My high-tide mark rose to the level of your breasts.

Carpets, like tentacles, wriggling down to the strand,
attracted passersby to the mouth of the clamor.
With lights and curtains, above the tedium
the bedrooms murmured in the grand hotels.

There are dark moments when our ballast gives out
from so much banging around. Moments, or centuries,
when the flesh revels in its nakedness and reels
to its own destruction, sucking the life from itself.

I groped around me, trying on your embrace,
but love was not where your embrace was.
I felt your hands stroking that physical ache
but a great nothing went before your hands.

Recorría, a lo largo, tu entrega desalmada,
por si había una cala donde tirar del copo,
por si acaso encontraba la voz del cenachero
aún mojada del brillo de los chanquetes vivos.

Era un lugar perdido para el Sur. El aroma
del moscatel tenía sinsabores de whisky.
Era un abrazo muerto, que llevo todavía
como un extraño objecto que la carne rechaza.

I searched, down the length of your soulless surrender,
for a calm bay where I could cast a net,
yearning to hear a trace of the vendor's voice
still wet with the glimmer of the flapping minnows.

It was a spoiled remnant of the South. The aroma
of muscatel was tainted with whiskey breath.
I carry that dead embrace inside me yet
like a foreign object the flesh tries to reject.

La ultima ternura

Hoy he vuelto al lugar, a las paredes
que me arropaban, tan calladamente,
aquel calor casi infantil, o mucho
más poderoso aún, y aquella
claridad mañanera, que nacía
de tus brazos en alto y del intento
de sujetarte el pelo.

He vuelto a aquel pedazo diminuto
de tiempo, que aún estaba
allí, como esperando, torpe, asido
al temblor de una cama
deshecha, a una mesita sin tapete
que se encogía en su humildad, a un vaso
que, en al opaco vidrio, cultivaba
alguno de esos trágicos momentos
de lucidez que en el amor existen.

He vuelto rastreando un rinconcito
del sol aquel, sin él, donde sentado,
acurrucado, sienta
llegar alta y despacio, hasta envolverme,
toda esa nada, o Dios, que me ha venido
persiguiendo, acosando, por los sitios
donde buscaba, lo que sólo existe
dentro de mí; lo que ahora, tarde, aprendo
que sólo estaba en mí y en mi otra forma
que eres tú, rodeando
mi soledad, como un gozoso espejo
que devolvía nuestra luz, y a un tiempo
nos aislaba del ruido y la existencia.

Hoy he vuelto por ver lo que me queda,
lo que ya no me queda, de la vasta

The Final Tenderness

Today I've come back to the place, to the walls
that swaddled, so quietly,
that almost boyish heat, or something
more passionate yet, and that clarity
of morning that shone
from your upraised arms as you worked
at pinning up your hair.

I've come back to that brief
stretch of time that still
was there, as if waiting, stuck there, poised
on the jigging edge
of an unmade bed, a table stripped of its cloth
and retiring into its modesty, a tumbler
that nurtured, within its opaque glass,
one of those tragic moments
of lucidity that occur in love.

I've come back following the trace
of a sunny corner, with no sun, where seated,
huddled, I feel
arriving—above and slowly—until it swallows me up,
all that nothingness, or God, that keeps on
following me, accosting me, through the places
I searched for what only exists
within myself: that which now, too late, I realize
was only in me and in my other self
which is you, surrounding
my loneliness like a lusty mirror
that sends us back our own light and at the same time
isolates us from sounds and from existence.

Today I've come back to see what's left to me,
What's no longer left to me, of the vast

ternura que, un momento,
sólo unos cortos siglos, entretuvo
mi corazón, aún tenso, suspendido
como un alud de llanto, entre los pliegues
de tus ropas tiradas en desorden;
como un alud de soledad, que cruje
renaciendo al milagro
devastador de un nuevo movimiento.

   Porque perder, cuando se pierde todo,
pues el amor es la unidad más dura,
nos separa del alma las pequeñas
cavidades amables,
esos huecos umbrosos, donde anida
todo lo grande y bello que en el hombre
necesita de la humedad, del vaho
animal que soporta
su condición donante, su indefensa
proyección a la entrega.

   Porque perder nos pone, desvalidos,
como cuando de niños
una visita nos echaba fuera
de nuestros juegos en la mesa grande
del comedor, nos pone,
sin saber cómo, en medio
de las frías ciudades, en los quicios
por donde pasan todos sin mirarnos,
nos sitúa perdidos y borrosos
en las lunas radiantes
de todos los comercios de la tierra.

   Hoy he vuelto al lugar, donde la vida
un día se me puso
de pie, donde bastaba
para vivir, oír caer la lluvia;
he vuelto a que me mires

tenderness that, one moment,
only a few short centuries, cheered
my heart, still tense there, suspended
like an avalanche of weeping, among the folds
of your clothes strewn about in disorder;
like an avalanche of loneliness that crackles
reborn in the devastating
miracle of another motion.

Because loss, when everything is lost,
well, love is the hardest thing of all;
it robs the soul of those tiny
intimate hollows,
those shady caves that are the nesting places
of all the great and beautiful that in a man
needs the moisture, the animal
vapor that supports
his readiness, his defenseless
giving of himself.

Because loss makes us insignificant,
as when we were children
and a social call drove us away
from our games at the big table
in the dining room; sets us,
we don't know how, in the midst
of cold cities, in doorways
where everyone walks by without looking at us,
situates us lost and cancelled out
in the radiant show windows
of all the commerce of the world.

Today I've come back to the place where life,
one day, set me
on my feet, when it was enough,
for a sense of being alive, to listen to the rain;
I've come back so you can look at me

desde donde no estás, desde esta almohada
donde tú ya no estás, y para siempre;
he vuelto tarde una vez más, y siento,
vencido al fin, que cuando se hace tarde
en el amor, no hay nada,
nunca habrá nada, ya, que nos redima.

from where you are no longer, from this pillow
where you are not, and forever;
I'm late again, and I understand,
finally convinced, that when we show up
late in love there's nothing,
there'll never be anything more, to redeem us.

Los esposos

Dame la mano; el cuerpo. Necesito
cruzar la calle. Dame
un tímido relámpago
de detrás de tus ojos, algo
que me sustente. Una palabra, un hijo
para cruzar la calle; dame un brazo
para correr. Ponte delante, así,
de cara a mí; que yo me vea cerca
reflejado. Y la mano
también. Dame la mano, el cuello joven,
el espejo, el cansancio
de ayer, el tiempo, sí,
dame el tiempo que te consuma, el peso
que hace posible tu llegada. Quiero
cruzar la calle. Dame
tu soledad, o más, la comisura
de tus labios, la piel de un muslo, algo
con que cubrirme. El gesto
que derrumba un deseo, algo sólido,
arañable, exterior, algo de ti
que arrope mi despegue.
Que no tengo más ancla, que no tengo
más posible contacto, que no tengo
más vertedero, o playa, o límite si quieres.
Dame el aliento, o lo que sea. Dame
algo que me acompañe.
Que está ya cerca el viento, que ya viene
por el árbol de al lado, y necesito
cruzar la calle. . . .

Spouses

Give me a hand, a body. I need
to go across. Give me
a timid flash
from behind your eyes, something
to hold me up. A word, a son
to go across; give me an arm
to run with. Stay there in front of me, like that,
face-to-face, so I can see myself
reflected. And your hand,
too. Give me your hand, your young throat,
a mirror, the fatigue
of yesterday, and time, yes,
give me the time that consumes you, the weight
that makes your presence possible. I want
to go across. Give me
your solitude, or better, the space
between your lips, the skin of a thigh, something
to cover me. The gesture
that flows from desire, something solid,
graspable, exterior, something yours
to prop up my rootlessness.
Because I have no other anchor, I have
no other contact possible, I have
no other bank, or beach, or limit, if you will.
Give me your breath, or whatever. Give me
something I can take with me.
For the wind moves closer, it's blowing
through that nearest tree now, and I need
to go across. . . .

Después del baile

A mí buscadme siempre
después del baile.
Cuando el salón vacío aún conserva
olor a carne perfumada, y gira
el recuerdo de una cintura airosa
sobre mesas y sillas en desorden.
Cuando el último ritmo aún perdura,
gratamente obsesivo, sin un cuerpo
en que posarse. Cuando Dios se acerca
por el túnel sin luz de este abandono.

A mí buscadme siempe
aquí, después del baile. Esta es la hora
de los que no llegaron a la fiesta.
Los enfundados, tristes, instrumentos
de la orquesta componen, en gris sucio,
el desolado dorso de la dicha.
Sobre este suelo ya es basura el vuelo
multicolor de los confeti, junto
al cigarro a medias apagado. Vasos,
botellas empezadas, restos
de esperanza inservible.
Entre este humo y soledad, aún queda
la vacía oquedad en donde hubo
una dura muchacha largamente
abrazada. Dios inventó esta fiesta
para darnos la dimensión exacta
de su silencio.

Este es mi sitio. Aquí me encontraréis.
Aquí en el centro de la pista, solo,
después del baile.

After the Ball

As for me, always look for me
after the ball.
When the empty ballroom still conserves
the fragrance of perfumed flesh, and the memory
of an airy waistline floats
over the disordered tables and chairs.
When the last beat still lingers,
pointlessly obsessive, without a body
to settle in. When God draws nearer
through this unlit tunnel of abandon.

For me, always look for me
here, after the ball. This is the hour
of those who didn't come to the party.
The sad packed-up instruments
of the orchestra form, in dirty gray,
the desolate underside of pleasure.
Over this floor the flight of multicolored confetti
is trash already, next to that cigarette
stubbed out half smoked. Glasses,
opened bottles, the remains
of a no-longer serviceable hope.
Within this smoke and solitude, there's still
the empty space in which a firm
young lady was endlessly embraced.
God invented this party
to give us the precise dimensions
of his silence.

This is my spot. You'll find me here.
Here, in the middle of the dance floor, alone.
After the ball.

Introducción al misterio

De la certeza de una realidad
que la razón no alcanza, ni el sentido;
del temor y el deseo;
de la oscura inminencia;
de la imaginación nace el misterio.

Entreabrimos la puerta y ya el crujido
de las maderas, y la resistencia
del herrumbroso gozne nos previene.
En la mansión no habitan
más que sombras y ruidos. ¿Quién los crea?
Lo primero es saber—y no es posible—
si tienen vida en sí, o los anima
nuestra presencia; si su ser genera
el pasmo o nos germina
de nuestro propio desconocimiento.
Sobre los ojos, en lo más sensible,
gravita la punzante
expectación.

Entramos.
La estancia es una inmensa
antesala, vacía
de no sabemos qué. Por las paredes
desnudas, no hay resquicio
en que colgar la fe que nos abriga.
Sólo una silla, en medio, reclamándonos.
Un crepitar de viejas
consejas, escuchadas junto al fuego,
sahuma el espesor de las tinieblas.
Espera que se puebla
de temerosas resonancias, formas
fantasmales, recuerdos
que provienen de un tiempo no pasado,

Introduction to Mystery

From the certainty of a reality
that reason can't encompass, or the senses;
from fear and desire;
from a dark imminence;
out of imagination mystery is born.

With the door only half open, already the creaking
of the boards and the resistance
of rust-caked hinges holds us back.
This mansion is inhabited by nothing
but shadows and sounds. Who creates them?
The first thing is to know—and it's not possible—
if they have life in themselves, or if they're animated
by our presence; if their being generates
this shuddering, or if it arises
from our own uncertainty.
Above the eyes, in the most sensitive spot,
we feel the prickling
expectation.

We go in.
The front room is an immense
waiting room, emptied
of we don't know what. Along
the bare walls there is no crevice
in which we can hang the faith that cloaks us.
Only a single chair in the center, beckoning.
A crepitation of ancient
fables, heard before the fire,
fumes through the dense obscurity.
We expect that it's populated
with frightful echoes, fantastic
forms, memories
proceeding from a time that never was,

que flotan desasidos, sin un hecho
anterior que los ate y origine.
El vacío se adensa y se coagula.

El misterio no está sobre nosotros.
El misterio nos cerca y nos oprime;
tal vez emane de nosotros mismos.
Altos ecos sin causa
rebotan por los ángulos oscuros
del salón. Intuiciones,
relumbres, tenues hálitos confusos
en los que la ansia cede ante el recelo.
Algo, que desemboca
después en una vana
crispación de impotencia y un extraño
dolor de no saber qué se nos pide.

Sentados en el centro, las pupilas
en vano dilatadas, pretendemos
hacer la luz frotando las preguntas.
Todo es inútil. Con temor y asombro
hemos llegado a la antesala, al borde.
Cederán las paredes, si empujamos,
pero no cambiarán las proporciones.
He ahí la consistencia del misterio.
Alas o soplos rozan
nuestra perplejidad desasistida.
¡Terrible parpadeo
de los ojos hundidos en lo negro!
Algo desconocido, desde el alto
mirador de su estado silencioso,
nos está contemplando.

that float detached, without
a previous act to originate and bind them.
The emptiness thickens and coagulates.

  The mystery is not above us.
The mystery surrounds and presses on us;
maybe it emanates from our very selves.
Shrill echoes without cause
resonate through the dark angles
of the salon. Intuitions,
flashes, tenuous crosscurrents
that move from anxiety to premonition:
something that erupts
finally in a groundless
twitching of impotence, and a strange
pain of not knowing what it wants of us.

  Seated in the center, our pupils
dilated in vain, we try
to shed a little light worrying at the questions.
It's all useless. With fear and awe
we've reached the anteroom, the border.
The walls will recede, if we push against them,
but the proportions will not change.
Here we have the consistency of mystery.
Wings, or gusts of air, brush
our floating perplexity.
  Terrible fluttering
of eyelids sunk in the blackness:
something unknown, from the high
perch of its silent condition,
is watching us.

Un gesto para el quinto aniversario de tu muerte

He venido hasta aquí por ver si el polvo
de lo que tanto amé,
por ver si esto que queda, que no es nada
de lo que tanto amé,
por ver si la corpórea cercanía
de un deshecho perfil amable, ay,
tantas veces descrito por los besos,
de unos huesos, o acaso de un vestido
que yo oprimía junto con tu brazo,
por ver si la certeza renovada
de este silencio en torno,
puede ponerle playas
a mi dolor, puede aún levantarse
como rocoso límite concreto
en donde rompa mi dolor.

Aquí, donde la nada se amontona,
y el jaramago crece en los vacíos
que dejó el pensamiento.
Aquí, donde los muertos, ordenados,
como puestos para secar y siempre
inútilmente cerca,
como las cosas entre sí, no tienen
tiempo y para hacer, tampoco para
dejar de hacer aquello que podría
ser comunicación, amor acaso.
Aquí, donde hasta el viento se arrincona,
después que el bieldo separó del grano
esto que sólo es paja,
aún menos que el polvillo de la paja.
Aquí, donde se asoma
la otra mano de Dios, la que sostiene
la esponja que nos borra,
donde la sombra sube

A Gesture for the Fifth Anniversary of Your Death

I've come here to see if the dust
of what I loved so much,
to see if whatever remains, which is nothing
of what I loved so much,
to see if the physical nearness
of an unmade lovable profile—ah,
how many times discovered with my kisses,
of a few bones, or maybe a dress
I squeezed once with your arm,
to see if the renewed certainty
of this enveloping silence
might give shores
to my grief, might even raise itself
like a concrete seawall
my pain could break against.

Here, where the nonexistent mounts
and wild mustard grows in the crevices
thought left behind.
Here, where the dead in their ranks,
as though laid out to dry, and always
uselessly near
like things juxtaposed, have no time
anymore for acting out
or not acting out whatever might
be communication, maybe even love.
Here, where even the wind skulks in the corners
after the winnower has separated from the grain
this which is only straw,
less even than the powdery dust of the straw.
Here, where the hand of God
hovers, the one that holds
the sponge that wipes us out,
where the spirit rises up

resumida en ciprés, pues de otro modo
no cabría en los cielos, ni en los hombres.

He venido hasta aquí, porque es domingo
y las calles con sol y las placetas
se llenan de muchachas
recién lavadas, blancas, y no puedo
con tanta vida, hoy que te recuerdo.
He venido porque los niños crecen
y crece el matorral y la luz crece
y lo bueno y lo malo crece, y todo
se expande y gira en torno de este punto
de dolorosa calma detenida.
He venido hasta aquí, sin más motivo
que el que tuviera de asomarme a un pozo
tan sólo porque es hondo,
o el de sentarme quedo junto al mar
porque es el mar. Y ahora
me pregunto si al cabo de este llanto,
si al cabo del dolor, no habrá un poquito
de tierra nada más,
de alguna imperceptible
materia tuya, que traspase el mármol
para tocar mi piel, para rozarme
levemente el cabello.
Porque nunca he querido
entender el amor sin una forma
de tacto. No he podido
renegar de este cuerpo que me diste.

He venido sin flores y sin luto.
He venido a fumarme este cigarro
delante de tu muerte;
solamente un cigarro, por aquello
que fue una gran borrasca de ternura.

reborn in cypresses, because if not
it wouldn't fit in heaven, nor in man.

I've come here because it's Sunday.
The sunny streets and the little squares
are filled with girls
freshly bathed, fair, and I can't deal
with so much life today, remembering you.
I've come here because the children are growing,
and the brambles are growing, and the light,
the good and the bad are growing, and it all
expands and whirls around this point
of sorrowful, suspended calm.
I've come here with no other motive
than whatever makes me look down a well
simply because it's deep,
or sit quietly beside the sea
because it's the sea. And now
I ask myself if, when all this sorrow is over,
at the end of the grief, there might not be
only a bit of earth,
some imperceptible matter
that's yours, that could pass through this marble
to touch my skin, gently
stroke my hair.
Because I've never wanted
to understand love without some kind
of touching. I've not been able
to deny this body you gave me.

I've come without flowers, not dressed in mourning.
I've come to smoke this cigarette
in front of your death;
only a cigarette, for all that
grand tempest of tenderness.

Ser un instante

La certidumbre llega como un deslumbramiento.
Se existe por instantes de luz. O de tiniebla.
Lo demás son las horas, los telones de fondo,
el gris para el contraste. Lo demás es la nada.

Es un momento. El cuerpo se deshabita y deja
de ser la transparencia con que se ve a sí mismo.
Se incorpora a las cosas; se hace materia ajena
y podemos sentirlo desde un lugar remoto.

Yo recuerdo un instante en que París caía
sobre mí con el peso de una estrella apagada.
Recuerdo aquella lluvia total. París es triste.
Todo lo bello es triste mientras exista el tiempo.

Vivir es detenerse con el pie levantado,
es perder un peldaño, es ganar un segundo.
Cuando se mira un río pasar, no se ve el agua.
Vivir es ver el agua; detener su relieve.

Mi vagar se acodaba sobre el pretil de hierro
del Pont des Arts. De súbito, centelleó la vida.
Sobre el Sena llovía y el agua, acribillada,
se hizo piedra, ceniza de endurecida lava.

Nada altera su orden. Es tan sólo un latido
del ser que, por sorpresa, llega a ser perceptible.
Y se siente por dentro lo compacto del hierro,
y somos la mirada misma que nos traspasa.

La lucidez elige momentos imprevistos.
Como cuando en la sala de proyección, un fallo
interrumpe la acción, deja una foto fija.
Al pronto el ritmo sigue. Y sigue el hundimiento.

To Be an Instant

Certitude comes as a bedazzlement,
instants of light. Or of blackness.
The rest is just hours passing, the backdrop,
gray for contrast. The rest is the void.

It's a moment. The body untenants itself, sets free
that transparency with which it can see itself.
It moves into things, materializes in matter,
and we can sense it from some distant place.

I remember an instant when Paris struck me
with the weight of a burnt-out star.
I remember that total rain. Paris is sad.
Everything lovely is sad while time exists.

To be alive is to pause with one foot lifted,
losing a step to gain a second.
Watching a river flow, we don't see the water.
To live is to see the water, to hold its patterns.

I was lazily propped on my elbows over the iron railing
of the Pont des Arts. Suddenly, life flashed out.
It was raining over the Seine and the water, riddled,
turned into stone, the ash of hardened lava.

Nothing alters its order. It's only one heartbeat
of a self which, by surprise, becomes perceptible.
And the density of iron is sensed from within,
and we become the glance that pierces us.

Lucidity always selects unforeseen moments,
as when in the projection room, a failure
interrupts the action, leaving a still shot.
The motion begins again, and we sink into it.

La pesada silueta del Louvre no se cuadraba
en el espacio. Estaba instalada en alguna
parte de mí, era un trozo de esa total conciencia
que hendía con su rayo la certeza absoluta.

Ser un instante. Verse inmerso entre otras cosas
que son. Después no hay nada. Después el universo
prosigue en el vacío su muerte giratoria.
Pero por un momento se detiene, viviendo.

Recuerdo que llovía sobre París. Los árboles
también eran eternos a la orilla. Al segundo,
las aguas reanudaron su curso y yo, de nuevo,
las miraba sin verlas, perderse bajo el puente.

The heavy silhouette of the Louvre
no longer took up space, but was installed
in some part of me, part of that total consciousness
split by a ray whose aim is absolute.

To be one instant. Yourself immersed in other
things that are. Afterward, nothing. The universe
continues its whirling death in the void.
But for one moment, it pauses, fully alive.

I remember that rain over Paris. Even the trees
on the banks became eternal. The next moment
the water renewed its course and once more I
watched it, seeing nothing, lose itself under the bridge.

Hoy no existe París

Hoy no existe París, porque estoy solo.
Hoy no es verdad toda esta luz, cernida
por los verdes castaños
del boulevard; no es cierta
esta gris claridad que lentamente
gotea; ni el mojado
paraguas que camina apresurado,
ni la mujer lejana, inexistente,
que me roza, dejándome
un poco de humedad cerca del hombro.

Hoy no existe París, porque no tengo
a quien decirle: "éstas son las piedras
de Saint Germain des Prés"; o sólo:
"rue Bonaparte"; o, acaso:
"aquella es la Cité"; o "éste es el Sena."
Y no tengo un portal, una escalera
donde esperar a alguien; y no puedo
impacientarme porque tarde alguien;
y quisiera poder decir a alguien:
"¿por qué tardaste?" o "¿qué hacemos ahora?"

Algo, una brizna de belleza, un tallo,
un pezón, una yema
que tímida se asoma entre el vaho infinito,
un poco nada más de luz, es mucho
para tan sólo un hombre en una calle.
Porque es extenso el reino inalcanzable
y cuando, alguna vez, se acerca y rasga
su veladura, convergiendo, como
los rayos a través de un prisma, en sólo
un pedazo de piel humana, es tanto
que convierte en pavesas
todo un presente, un cuerpo, un desamparo.

Today Paris Doesn't Exist

Today Paris doesn't exist, because I'm alone.
Today it isn't real, all this light filtered
through the green chestnut trees
of the boulevard; there's nothing certain
in this gray clarity that slowly
drizzles, the damp
umbrella passing by so hastily,
that distant woman, nonexistent,
who brushes me, leaving
a little moisture near my shoulder.

Today Paris doesn't exist, because there's no one
to whom I can say, "These are the stones
of Saint Germain des Prés" or, simply,
"rue Bonaparte," or maybe
"That's the Cité," or "This is the Seine."
And I don't have a doorway, a staircase,
where I could wait for someone. I can't
grow impatient because someone's late.
I'd like to say to somebody,
"Why are you so late?" or "What shall we do now?"

Anything, a fragment of beauty, a sprout,
a stem, a shoot
timidly pushing up through the infinite fog,
nothing more than a little light is a lot
for a man so alone on a street.
Because this ungraspable distance is so great
and when, sometimes, it closes in, unveiling
its tinted layers, converging like
a ray split by a prism, on merely
a bit of human skin, it's enough
to burn a body, an entire
presence, down to ashes, a derelict.

Sobre los techos de París, ondea
mi corazón como un deshilachado
estandarte. Columnas
de ruido ascienden de las plazas. Bullen
miradas, pechos, íntimos encajes
detrás de las persianas, por las altas
buhardillas. Y estoy fuera.
Y estoy perdido y fuera y anochece.
Barbotea la vida como en una
redoma inmensa y yo la miro, inmóvil,
abrazando al cristal, externo, y nada
me da de su calor.
                        Por las aceras
nadie saca una mano del brillante
impermeable, nadie
asoma una palabra a la que pueda
asirme para andar. Y el gris se adensa.
Y los anuncios que se encienden hacen
más palpable la irrealidad, más cerca.

Hoy no existe París porque estoy solo.
Porque la gente gesticula dentro
de las lunas de los cafés, en medio
de la prisa del metro, y yo no tengo
una voz cerca que me diga algo
como "sigue lloviendo," o "¿que día es hoy?";
una voz que pueda
templar un poco esta frialdad cortante.
Tanta belleza es nada
y qué más da, si se anda así pegado
a las paredes, solo, recogiendo
murmullos por los parques, vida ajena,
aliento ajeno que se va y no alcanza
a empañar nuestros mínimos cristales.

Over the roofs of Paris my heart
wavers like a frayed
banner. Columns
of sound rise up from the squares, a rustle
of glances, breasts, intimate laces
behind the blinds, through the high
dormers. And I'm outside.
I'm lost and outside and it's growing dark.
Life is bubbling over as though
an immense flask contained it, and I watch, immobile,
hugging the glass, banished, and nothing
gives me its warmth.
                              Out on the sidewalk
no one holds out a hand from
the impenetrable splendor, no one
ventures a word that might set me
in motion. And the grayness thickens
and the signs as they light up make the unreality
more palpable, bring it nearer.

Today Paris doesn't exist, because I'm alone.
Because people gesture behind
the café windows, in the midst
of the bustling subway, and I have
no voice nearby that might say something
like *It's still raining* or *What day is today?*
—a voice which might
temper this biting coldness.
So much beauty is nothing
and what's it worth, wandering this way, huddled
against the walls, alone, collecting
murmurs in the parks, alien life,
alien breath that blows away
without even fogging my glasses.

La tierra, una ciudad, un charco, el cerco
que illumina un farol, es demasiado
cuando no se comparte, cuando sirve
de fondo a tanto andar, a pedir tanto,
a tanta soledad.

The earth, a city, a puddle, the sphere
illuminated by a street lamp is too much
when it isn't shared, when it serves in the end
only for so much walking, so much wanting,
so much loneliness.

Un bar en América

La noche acompasaba mi descenso.
Sólo un bar encontré, de tanto mapa
pensado desde arriba;
un bar del otro lado de la esfera.
Me rodeaban mesas frías, como
trozos de hielo sobre el agua.
Un bar del otro lado de mis cosas,
del otro lado de mi almohada blanda.
Dos camareros blancos ordenaban
apresuradamente la penumbra.

Pero había una mujer allí, visible,
una mujer, quisás vestida, suave,
instalada en un lado
del escaso calor que aún me quedaba.

Me detuve delante de la copa,
delante de la tierra. Fue en el centro
de América, bajando
por la Florida, y luego a la derecha.
Era un bar con ventanas, y en la parte
de afuera estaba el tiempo.

Y yo me preguntaba si es que habría
una sola mujer en todo el mundo
con las piernas cruzadas;
una sola presencia que pudiera
abrirse paso en medio de la niebla.

Afuera bostezaban las hambrientas
avenidas; porteros
enguantados cerraban
todas las puertas. Fue cuando las notas
de un "mariachi" brotaron del absurdo.

A Bar in America

The night guided my descent.
I only found one bar, out of a whole map
studied from above;
a bar on the other side of the globe.
Empty tables surrounded me, frigid
as chunks of floating ice.
A bar on the other side of my concerns,
on the other side of my soft pillow.
Two waiters in white bustled about
putting the shadows in order.

But there was a woman, visible,
a woman, dressed somehow or other, suave,
sitting there at the outer edge
of the little warmth I'd kept with me.

I sat in front of my drink,
in front of the earth. I was in the middle
of the Americas, heading down
for Florida, and then to the right.
It was a bar with windows
and outside them was the weather.

And I wondered if there were really
only one woman in all the world
with her legs crossed so;
only one single presence able
to open a path through the fog.

Outside the hungry avenues
were yawning; gloved
doormen attended
all the entrances. Then the notes
of a "Mariachi" band burst into the absurd.

Multicolores taxis hilvanaban
una alfombra de ruidos dolorosos.
Entré en el bar como en la muerte. Pude
recostar mi mirada sobre el brillo
de la pulida solería,
introducir mis manos en la dulce
templanza de la media luz. La copa,
sólo la copa, unía
lo que de mí quedaba con el hombre
que empezó a caminar, desde el descanso
del aire conocido.

Pero había una mujer, tal vez callada,
que sostenía con su cuerpo el borde
animal de mi pena. Y era triste,
lo recuerdo, mirarla
tan cerca del olvido.

Por vez primera estaba solo. Estaba
físicamente solo; es tan palpable
como estar empapado, o dolorido.
La soledad empieza a las seis horas
de vuelo, o las veinte
noches de barco. Entonces se concentra
y pesa en nuestras ropas, y congela
nuestras palabras al salir. Por eso
el bar se recogió sobre sí mismo,
como un extraño caracol, sintiendo
que un hombre solo entraba.
El bar era una gruta en el espacio,
una pequeña gruta con tibieza.

Pero había una mujer, que me ignoraba
desde todos los ángulos. Estaba
sentada, quizás viva,
por los alrededores de mi pasmo.

Multicolored taxis laid down
a carpet of painful noise.
Entering that bar was like walking into death.
I could rest my gaze on the gleam
of the polished floor,
move my hands through the soft
tepidness of the half-light. The drink,
only the drink, united
what was left of me with the man
who began this journey, away from the consolation
of my familiar surroundings.

But there was a woman, quiet maybe,
whose body defined the outlines
of my brute misery. And it was sad,
I remember, to look at her
so close to being forgotten.

For the first time, I was alone. I was
alone, physically; it's as palpable
as being drenched, or in pain.
That isolation begins after six hours
of flight, or twenty
nights on a ship. Then it condenses
and weighs down our clothes, and freezes
our words as they come out. And so
the bar spiraled around itself
like a strange snail, sensing
that a man had come in alone.
The bar was a cranny in space,
a tiny cranny with a bit of warmth.

But there was a woman, who ignored me
from all angles. She was
sitting there, lively maybe, in the space
that marked off my desolation.

Entonces las paredes, el silencio,
unos pasos cansados, o el sonido
de alguna cucharilla
en el cristal de vaso, entonces, digo,
las cortinas plegadas, o un cigarro
apagado en el suelo, y, sobre todo,
la conciencia del mar, o la de aquellas
movibles nubes pardas
que me acechaban, o las cordilleras
que interceptaban mis recuerdos,
entonces los océanos del miedo,
las tormentas del llanto,
giraban y giraban, y en su vértice
flotaba yo, aferrado
a la tabla de un bar, sólo un pedazo
de madera o crisal de bar, o whisky,
en el centro del mundo.

Pero había una mujer, sentada, cierta,
no recuerdo si sola, tal vez lejos,
pero había una mujer, en algún sitio,
y sus piernas formaban un perfecto
ángulo recto con mi soledad.

And then the walls, the silence,
some heavy footsteps, or the tinkle
of a spoon against the side
of a glass; then, I say,
the pleated drapes, or a cigarette stubbed out
on the floor, and more than anything else
a sense of the sea, those drifting
dark clouds closing in
on me, or the chain of mountains
that interrupted my memories;
then the oceans of fear,
the storms of anguish
whirled and whirled around me, as I floated there
in the eye of the storm, hanging on
to the edge of the bar, only a scrap
of wood, or glass, of a bar, or whiskey,
in the center of the world.

But there was a woman, seated, sure of herself.
I don't remember if she was alone, maybe at a distance,
but there was a woman, in some spot or other,
and her legs formed a perfect
right angle to my loneliness.

Vuelve un amigo

Vuelve un amigo y deja
sobre la mesa su mirada limpia,
su ávida manera
de ir recogiendo, como
de pico a pico, las palabras
premiosas
con que arropamos el encuentro.

Vuelve un amigo antiguo
lleno de barcos, luces
de ciudades remotas, islas; trae
selváticas lianas, entresecas,
enmarañadas en el pelo; viene
más lento, como bajo el peso
de mucho andar.
                         Es él, aquí otra vez.
El mismo. Y es la misma
su voz; pretende ser el mismo
todo el contorno que la vida ha ido
diluyendo. Y hablando, le buscamos
por el rostro, mirando abiertamente,
los perfiles de un cambio que no trata
de ocultar.
                         Es ésta su figura,
amable como antes, acaso
levemente vencida, que ahora
es inestable, como
si ocupase un espacio
que ya no es suyo, aunque siga siendo
suyo. Adivinamos
el sesgo de un entonces
que se perdió y, de nuevo,
desalentadamente persiguimos.

A Friend Comes Back

A friend comes back and leaves
his fresh gaze on the table,
his nervous way
of choosing, as though
one at a time,
the carefully selected words we need
for softening the encounter.

An old friend comes back
full of ships, the lights
of distant cities, islands; he brings
jungle vines, half dried,
tangled in his hair; he moves
more slowly, as if under the weight
of much walking.
                        Here he is again.
The same. And his voice
is the same; a whole presence
that life has been melting down
tries to be the same. And as we talk
we search his face, watching frankly
for signs of a change he doesn't try
to hide.
                The form is his,
charming as always, maybe
a little uneasy, a bit
unstable, as if
it occupied a space
no longer its own, although it still
belongs to him. We try to retrace
the outlines of another time
that's been lost, and distractedly
pick up the thread again.

El aire que desplaza no es el aire
del día aquel centellante
en el que la memoria se debate
por arribar. En el momento mismo
del desembarco, todo un continente
se fue a otros mares.
                          Blandas
formas de nada; hoscas, suspendidas
cavernas, altos
desfiladeros donde hierve el vértigo.
Y todo sigue igual.
Y basta un paso, un ¡hola!, una mirada
que resume unos años y los tacha.

     Vuelve un amigo y es como un bocado
de pan,
como el crujir caliente y olvidado
de la redonda hogaza familiar;
es como
coger de nuevo un libro, que leímos
alguna vez, que sigue
diciéndonos lo mismo, aunque los ojos
ya son otros, aunque el texto
se fue cambiando, él solo, en los estantes.
Regresa y con él viene,
como tenuemente adherido a lo gastado
de sus hombros, aquello
que se nos fue muriendo mientras tanto,
que aún llevamos dentro y ya está muerto.
     No se interpone nada en el encuentro.
No se interpone nada
entre la doble fiesta, entre el estruendo
de la alegría, sólo
una insensible pátina herrumbrosa
de tiempo, que no es nada,
que es todo, que no vemos,
que no queremos ver y que prosigue
su destrucción, en medio del abrazo.

The air he displaces is not the air
of that sparkling day
the memory struggles
to take port in. The very moment
he took ship, a whole continent
went off to other seas.
                              Blurred
unreal forms, gloomy suspended
caverns, high
canyon rims where vertigo shakes us.
And everything is the same.
A step is enough, a hello, a look
that sums up the years and wipes them out.

    A friend comes back, and it's like a mouthful
of bread,
like the crackling-hot and forgotten
round family loaf;
it's like
picking up a book again that we read
one time, and that still
says the same, but our eyes
have changed, and the book itself
has changed, changed itself, there on the shelf.
He comes back and with him comes,
as though lightly attached to the slump
of his shoulders, something
that died in us a long time ago,
that we still carry within us, but it's dead.
    Nothing interferes in the encounter.
Nothing interferes
in this dual celebration, in the manifestations
of joy; only
an insensible rusty patina
of time, that's nothing,
but it's everything, that we don't see,
that we don't want to see, and that achieves
its destruction, in the midst of the embrace.

Tornado

En esta tarde en que el silencio medra,
caigo de aquí otra vez. Tornado y solo,
algo también rozado
el sobre por los bordes, me recibo,
como devuelto así por el cartero,
de tanto amigo a donde fui y no abrieron,
o se encontraba ausente, o qué sé yo, de tanto
buzón oscuro, tanto caldeado
ragazo en balde y mira aquí este sello
en mi piel, esta marca
de sangre: devolver al remitente.

¿Cejar? ¿Morir? ¿O hacerse
cequia de nuevo y vuelta con la aceña
que nada muele ya sino a sí misma?
¿Ahechar cuando no hay trigo y, sobre nada,
despedirse otra vez, y otro retorno,
y otra misiva a nadie? Hoy ya basta.

Arde en el llar el sobre
sin abrir, que me sé su cantilena,
y mira se retuerce y quién negara,
después de casi todo,
que humo y cardeña llegue más seguro.

Total, en esta tarde
mezquina y para qué, larga si menos,
aún queda tiempo para verse ascua,
rescoldo propio.
                    Al fin, si se deviene
desde perder, pues, ya perdido, acaso
—es por hablar, digamos—
una chispa, un fulgor, no sé, podria. . . .

Sent Back

On this afternoon that gathers a hoard of silence
I fall back here again. Sent back and alone,
the envelope a little frayed
around the edges, I receive myself
as if returned by the postman
from so many friends I went to, and they didn't open
or weren't at home, or how do I know, from so many
dark mailboxes, so much cuddly warmth
down the drain, and look at this stain
on my skin, this blood-red
mark: Return to Sender.

Give up? Die? Or dig
another ditch and start up the mill
that no longer grinds anything but itself?
Sift air, since there's no grain, for nothing,
start out again, and another return,
and another message to nobody? Today, enough yet.

The envelope burns in the grate
unopened; I know every word of its tune
and I watch it writhe, and who can deny
that it's more likely to get there,
in the almost end, as smoke and flying ashes.

In short, on this miserly afternoon,
and why not—it's long if nothing else—
there's still time left to see my life as embers,
my own cinders.
                And then, since it's come back
from being lost, well, lost already, maybe
—just for the sake of saying something, let's say—
a spark, a glow, I don't know, maybe it could. . . .

Donde sonó una risa

Donde sonó una risa, el el recinto
del aire, en los pasillos transparentes
del aire donde, un día,
sonó una risa azul, tal vez dorada,
queda por siempre un hueco, un lienzo triste,
un muro acribillado, un arco roto,
algo como el desgaire de una mano
cansada, como un trozo
de madera podrida en una playa.

Donde saltó la vida y luego nada,
y el corazón, de un golpe,
echó a rodar, y luego nada, queda
una cama deshecha,
un cuarto clausurado, un portón viejo
en el vacío, algo
como un andén cubierto por la arena;
queda por siempre el hueco
que deja un estampido por el bosque.

De bruces, husmeando, rastreando
unas huellas, tirando
del hilo de un perfume,
penetra el corazón por galerías
que un latido de sangre subterránea
horadó alguna vez y allí quedaron.
Y que allí permanecen con su húmeda
oscuridad de tigres en acecho.
Penetra el corazón a tientas, llama
y su misma llamada lo sepulta.

Donde sonó una risa, una vidriera,
una delgada lámina de espacio

Where Laughter Once Rang Out

    Where laughter once rang out, in the precincts
of air, in the transparent passageways
of air where, one day,
laughter rang out blue, or perhaps golden,
forever there remains an interval, a sad canvas,
a pocked wall, a broken arch,
something like the limp gesture
of a weary hand, like a piece
of driftwood on a beach.

    Where life leaped up, and then nothing,
and a heart, all at once,
began to race, and then nothing, there remains
an unmade bed,
a sealed-up room, an old portal
in the void, something like
a station platform covered with sand;
forever there remains that interval
left by a shot fired through the woods.

    Nose down, sniffing, searching out
tracks, grasping
a thread of scent,
the heart goes burrowing through galleries
a subterranean current of blood
excavated and left there.
And they continue there with the humid
darkness of tigers in wait.
The heart goes burrowing, groping, calling out
and its own cry inters it.

    Where laughter once rang out, a windowpane,
a thin sheet of space,

estalló lentamente. Y no es posible
poner de nuevo en orden tanta ruina.

Un nuevo aliento merodea. Llegan
otros sonidos hasta el borde y piden
su momento para existir. Afluyen
nuevas formas de vida
que al final toman cuerpo y se acomodan.
Pero el tiempo ya es otro y el espacio
ya es otro y no es posible
revivir lo que el tiempo desordena.

En la cresta del agua o de la espuma
donde una risa naufragó, ya nada
podrá buscar, hundirse, hallar los restos,
nadie podrá decir: éste es el sitio.
El mar no tiene sitios y sus cimas
son instantes de brillo y se disuelven.

Pero quedan los huecos, queda el tiempo.
El tiempo es un conjunto
de irrellenables huecos sucesivos.
Donde sonó una risa queda un hueco,
un coágulo de nada, una lejana
polvareda que fue,
que ya no está, pero que sigue hablando,
diciendo al alma que, en alguna parte,
algo cruzó al galope y se ha perdido.

exploded slowly. And it's not possible
to put such ruin back in order again.

A new breath comes marauding. Other
sounds arrive at the verge and plead
for their moment of existence, a flood
of new forms of life
that finally take shape, assume their places.
But time is already other, and space
is already elsewhere, and it's not possible
to live again what time has disordered.

On the crest of a wave, in the spume
where laughter foundered, there's no longer
anything to seek, to sink, no remains to discover;
no one can say: this is the site.
The sea has no sites and its summits
are moments that shine and dissolve.

But the interval remains, time remains.
Time is a gathering together
of unfillable successive hollows.
Where laughter once rang out, an interval remains,
a curd of nothing, a distant
cloud of dust that was
and is no more, but it keeps on speaking,
telling the spirit that somewhere
something passed by on the run and disappeared.

El miedo, no

El miedo, no. Tal vez, alta calina,
la posibilidad del miedo, el muro
que puede derrumbarse, porque es cierto
que detrás está el mar.
El miedo, no. El miedo tiene rostro,
es exterior, concreto,
como un fusil, como una cerradura,
como un niño sufriendo,
como lo negro que se esconde en todas
las bocas de los hombres.
El miedo, no, Tal vez sólo el estigma
de los hijos del miedo.

Es una angosta calle interminable
con todas las ventanas apagadas.
Es una hilera de viscosas manos
amables, sí, no amigas.
Es una pesadilla
de espeluznantes y corteses ritos.
El miedo, no. El miedo es un portazo.
Estoy hablando aquí de un laberinto
de puertas entornadas, con supuestas
razones para ser, para no ser,
para clasificar la desventura,
o la ventura, el pan, o la mirada
—ternura y miedo y frío—por los hijos
que crecen. Y el silencio.
Y las ciudades rutilantes, huecas.
Y la mediocridad, como una lava
caliente, derramada
sobre el trigo, y la voz, y las ideas.

Not Fear

Not fear. Maybe, out there somewhere,
the possibility of fear; the wall
that might tumble down, because it's for sure
that behind it is the sea.
Not fear. Fear has a countenance;
it's external, concrete,
like a rifle, a shot bolt,
a suffering child,
like the darkness that's hidden
in every human mouth.
Not fear. Maybe only the brand
of the offspring of fear.

It's a narrow, interminable street
with all the windows darkened,
a thread spun out from a sticky hand,
friendly, yes, not a friend.
It's a nightmare
of polite ritual wearing a fright wig.
Not fear. Fear is a door slammed in your face.
I'm speaking here of a labyrinth
of doors already closed, with assumed
reasons for being, or not being,
for categorizing bad luck
or good, bread, or an expression
—tenderness and panic and frigidity—for the children
growing up. And the silence.
And the cities, sparkling, empty.
And the mediocrity, like a hot
lava, spewed out over
the grain, and the voice, and the idea.

No es el miedo. Aún no ha llegado el miedo.
Pero vendrá. Es la conciencia doble
de que la paz también es movimiento.
Y lo digo en voz alta y receloso.
Y no es el miedo, no. Es la certeza
de que me estoy jugando, en una carta,
lo único que pude,
tallo a tallo, hacinar para los hombres.

It's not fear. The real fear hasn't come yet.
But it will. It's the doublethink
that believes peace is only another movement.
And I say it with suspicion, at the top of my lungs.
And it's not fear, no. It's the certainty
that I'm betting, on a single card,
the whole haystack I've piled up,
straw by straw, for my fellow man.

Piedra-libre

Por el jardín agazapados, cada
uno en su puesto y solos,
niños a piedra-libre, tras un seto,
tras una adelfa, hombres
a idea y a palabra libre, ocultos
en lo oscuro, detrás de un nombre, cerca
y dispersos, detrás de cada oficio,
y el que se queda, escudriñando, ¡visto!
desde su privilegio,
desde su luz mentida—ya ha contado
hasta diez—desde el mando, poseyendo
la valla, sus derechos,
la vastedad de su dominio.
                                    Miro
los arbustos, la sombra
del escondite que me ampara, el alto
murallón que me cerca. Miro el hueco
por donde acechan los fusiles. Miro
un claro entre dos sauces
y un niño ¡visto! que se cruza y sale
cabizbajo y mohino
hacia la luz. Miro mi propia sombra
que puede delatarme; salto quedo
de un rosal a una yuca, de un silencio
a una coartada.
                          Reptan,
se acercan ¡visto! van cayendo algunos;
el foco barre la memoria, dejan
el resguardo de la mimosa, pasos
hasta la adelfa, gateando, hurtan
los barrotes, el miedo, se guarecen
tras de la alheña ¡visto! aquél resiste
la tortura.

Hide-and-Seek

Crouched throughout the garden, each
alone in his spot,
children at hide-and-seek, behind a fence,
behind an oleander, men at seeking
freedom of speech and thought, hidden
in the dark, behind a name, in groups
or scattered, behind every calling,
and the one who's "it" peering around—I spy!—
from his privilege,
from his false light—already he's counted up
to ten—from the seat of command, holding
the fort, his laws,
the vastness of his dominion.
                              I watch
the bushes, the shade
of the hiding place that protects me, the high
wall that surrounds me, and a hole
where a rifle might be waiting. I see
a space between two willows
and a boy—I spy!—who comes out
crestfallen and scowling
into the light. I look at my own shadow
that could give me away, hop without a sound
from a rosebush to a yucca, from a silence
to an alibi.
                  They creep on their bellies,
they're getting closer—I spy!—some are falling;
that eye like a searchlight sweeping
through the mind; they quit
the safety of the mimosa, steal a few inches
to the oleander. Pattern of jail bars. The fear. They take refuge
behind a privet—I spy!—that one
holds up under the torture.

Tumbado sobre el césped
espero y miro, avanzo con los codos,
¡ahora! me incorporo,
me juego el juego ¡visto! ya no hay tiempo,
corro entre los disparos, atravieso
el clamorero, saltos
de alegría infantil, de un quiebro evito
la última redada, el árbol último,
salvo la valla y grito, casi lloro:
"¡Piedra-libre para mí, y para todos
mis compañeros!"

Hugging the ground,
I watch and wait, scooting on my elbows,
and now! I give it everything
I've got, I'm game for the game—I spy!—time's
running out, I dodge between the shots, daring
the giveaway capers and screams
of childish excitement, with one twist I'm past
the last trap, the last tree,
I've won home base, and I shout, almost crying,
"Home free for me and for everyone
on my side!"

Como si fuera un hombre

Como si fuera un punto, solamente
una mota de humanidad, un gramo
del deshonor del mundo, andando,
pesadamente andando por el valle; un punto
donde gravita el vértice invertido
de una pirámide de muertos;
cansadamente andando por el valle,
como si fuera el valle la campiña
feliz donde los trigos,
los altos trigos del amor, mecían
la redonda certeza sucesiva
de una palabra sola: "mañana," y donde el álamo
de la ribera alzaba su costumbre
de acumular belleza, hoy vertida
sobre la cara del espanto; andando,
desmadejadamente andando por la tierra,
como si fuera parte de la tierra
y siguiesen sus venas abajo, por la tierra,
buscando, persiguiendo, pidiendo
la comunicación con otros hombres
que apostados enfrente, silenciosos,
como si fueran hombres, lo acarician
desde la mira del fusil; andando
por el musgo, y la era, y las hormigas,
por los surcos de los arados, solo,
un hombre oscurecido, deslizante,
como una voz gritada desde un monte,
como una pulsación, como el deshielo
de la ternura, avanza,
avanza solo por el valle.

Como si fuera la razón el eco
ramificado de los mil temblores
que conmueven las fibras, palmo a palmo,

As If There Were a Man

As if there were a point, only
a mote of humanity, a grain
of the dishonor of the world, walking,
heavily walking down the valley: the center
of gravity of the inverted tip
of a pyramid of the dead;
walking exhausted down the valley,
as though the valley were the gay
countryside where the wheat,
the waving wheat stalks of love, rocked
the round successive certainty
of a single word: "tomorrow," and where the cottonwoods
along the riverbank offered up their way
of accumulating beauty, now spilled out
over the face of horror; walking,
languidly walking over the earth,
as if he were part of the earth,
and his veins grew downward, into the earth,
seeking, pursuing, begging for
communication with other men,
who, posed in front of him, silent,
as if they were men, salute him
from the sight of a rifle; walking
through the moss, and the threshing field, and the ants,
through the plowed furrows, alone,
a man in shadow, wavering,
like a voice shouted from a mountaintop,
like a pulsation, like a melting
tenderness, advances,
advances alone down the valley.

As if reason were an echo
branching from the thousand tremblings
that move the fibers, end to end,

de una piel que ha servido,
que sirve para el labio, que se tensa
como si fuera piel humana, y fuera
propicia todavía
para el roce temido del recuerdo
perseguidor; y todo
como si fuera flor de una explosión
total que se propaga por las cuencas
donde estuvo el amor, sin más fronteras
que el humo y los lamentos; avanzando,
y un paso y otro paso, en la armonía
del valle atardecido, donde acampa
la desventura universal, del valle
fosa convulsa, cúmulo de espasmos,
un hombre sigue por el polvo.

    Él, tenía un caballo.
Él tenía una parra ante la puerta.
El pozo estaba cerca de su casa, a un lado
de la puerta empedrada de su casa.

    Avanza, seco, por el valle.
Como si fuera la justicia el vaho
que sale de una herida. Pasa
sobre cuerpos tirados, que aún exhiben
los dos ojos abiertos, como clavos
que los sujetan a la muerte. Y pasa
como si fuera cierta toda aquella
envoltura sedosa, y toda aquella
gesticulante y tibia pátina elocuente
que envuelve los motivos,
que va poniendo nombres
gloriosos al disparo y la gangrena,
como si fueran ya otros nombres
extraños padre y madre, y fuera
distinto lumbre, o cántaro, y otra cosa
fuera decir: "te espero junto al roble."
Cada paso en el valle le devuelve

of the skin that has served,
that serves for a lip, that contracts
as though it were human skin, were
still disposed
to feel the faint touch
of the memory that clings to it; and everything
as if it were the bloom of a total explosion
that bursts through the sockets
where the eyes of love once were, with no frontiers
but smoke and lamentation; advancing,
and a step, and another step, in the harmony
of the valley at afternoon, where the universal
catastrophe is camped, the convulsed grave
of the valley, a heap of shudders,
a man continues through the dust.

Him, he had a horse.
He had grapevines beside his door.
The well was near the house, to one side
of the stone-paved entry to his house.

He advances, arid, down the valley.
As though justice were the ooze
that seeps from a wound. He moves along
over strewn corpses whose two eyes
are still open, like spikes
nailing them to death. And he goes by
as if they were dependable,
all those silky wrappings, and all
that cooing theatrical eloquence
that cloaks the motives,
that goes on giving glorious names
to shooting and gangrene,
as if there were other new words
for saying *Father* and *Mother*,
and *firelight* or *water jug* meant something else,
or *I'll meet you by the oak tree* had a new meaning.
Every step he takes through the valley points up

la repugnanza de la tierra.
Cada estampido le cercena un poco
de la niñez. Un grito, como un géiser
hirviente y repentino, se levanta
muy cerca de sus pies. La tarde opone
almohadones de sangre a los sonidos.

Como si fuera la locura el nudo
donde confluye todo pensamiento,
y se anudase en las gargantas
sin más salida, o cauce, que el vesánico
paso que avanza, y fuera
la fiebre, finalmente, el móvil último
de toda la teoría alucinante
de tácticas, y fuera
el pasmo, y suma y sigue,
y el asco, y el desprecio
la consecuencia de seguir, y el hombre
como si fuera todo carne y sólo
carne el hombre, y luego,
y más abajo, a la altura misma
de los sollozos,
como si fuera Dios la cruel luciérnaga
que destella impasible junto al hoyo
de los obuses, todo
como si fuera del revés y siempre,
porque siempre es ahora, en este instante
que es el instante del delirio, y como
si fuera, por ser algo, verdadero
todo lo dicho de la patria, y fuera
la verdad de la historia la que pesa
sobre los hombres, hoy, eternamente,
un hombre muerto avanza por el valle.

Como si fuera un hombre y fuera un valle.
Comi si fuera el frío de una loca
carcajada de Dios, que avanza, humana,
por el valle.

the repugnance of the earth.
Every shot robs him of a little
of his childhood. A sudden scream
boils up like a geyser,
almost beneath his feet. The afternoon
stifles the sound with cushions of blood.

    As if it were madness, the knot
where thought is united,
and were stuck in our throats like a lump
with no exit or pathway but the half-crazy
step that advances, and as if a fever,
finally, were the ultimate cause
of all the brilliant theory
of tactics, and convulsion
and so on and so forth
and the turned stomach, and scorn were
the consequence of going on, and man
as if he were all body and nothing
but a body, and then,
and lower yet, at the level
of sobs,
as if God were a cruel firefly
flickering indifferent above the pit
where the cannons are, and everything
as if it were turned inside out and forever,
because forever is now, in this moment
which is the moment of delirium, and as if
everything that's said about the fatherland
were, for the sake of being something, true, as if
it were the truth of history that weighs down
on his shoulders, today, eternally,
a dead man advances through the valley.

    As if there were a man and a valley.
As if it were the chill of a crazy
guffaw of God that advances, in human form,
through the valley.

Oleo

No el chasquido rebenque
de los ojos, ni mucho
la mueca amojamada, la cadente
baba senil, ni el tiemblo vagoroso
dentro del entorchado, no, ni el lelo
parpadeo.
                    Debajo
de la cáscara nuez, cerebro activo
engrasado con líquidos
de muertos incontables, más abajo
y horizontal en la mirada, afloro
en el hondón vacío
que dejó la conciencia, apunta un algo
de todo desamor, de un odio todo
que revierte de sí, que se refleja
en cada enfrente de temor, en cada
sumisa cabezada.
                              No la mano
colgante, pretendida
sin voluntad, ni tanto la tiesura
acartonada, no, ni el dengue
silabear la gratitud mentida.

De un detrás de la chepa
recompuesta, de un fondo descompuesto
de expolio, de una charca,
de un más allá de moribundos lívidos
que mueven las cortinas, que se agarran
a los retratos, más allá, en un lado
inmemorial, despunta
una ausencia letal, un no haber sido
que espanta, una carencia
de realidad temible que incorpora

Oil

Not the cracking whip
of the eyes, not even the fishy
smile, hard and dry as jerky, the pendent
senile drool, nor the slight twitching
the gold braid almost hides, no, not
the idiotic tic.
                              Underneath
that nutshell, a restless mind
greased with the fluids
of uncountable dead; down a little
and level with the gaze, in the furze
of the empty pit
conscience left behind, glitters a kind of
total disaffection, a global hatred
that falls back on itself, that's reflected
in every fearful countenance,
in every servile bow.
                              Not
the relaxed hand, a pretense
of casualness, not so much
the cardboard stiffness, no, nor the prissy
spelling out a lying gratitude.

From somewhere behind the hump
the collar supports, from a crater without
supports, razed to the ground, from a sinkhole,
an out there of the livid walking dead
who rustle the curtains, who claw
at the pictures, out there, in the immemorial
slime, arises a lethal
nonpresence, a having never been
anything but a ghost, a fearful
unreality that invests

al acervo historial un nuevo espacio
en blanco—no hay más sangre:
que la busquen, a ver, por todo el reino—
que incorpora una nueva
laguna atemporal, mientras las palmas
clausuran y se esfuma,

sin más, la repetida ceremonia.

the heritage of history with a new
blank space—there's no blood left:
search the whole land and you'll see—
that creates a new hiatus
outside of time, as the air repeats
and repeats the applause that cheers
the broken record of the ceremony.

Farándula

Cuando te sientas en tu ¿ya? poltrona
de madurez y miras
por encima del hombro, pasos, antes,
de oficial, una alcayata
para agarrarse a la pared, subiendo,
después los hijos, tal vez no, la tregua
de decirte tener un por si acaso,
y más después la cana
primera y te interrogas
¿qué es de mí? . . .
        Se te muestra
tu desvaída imagen, con contornos
de qué temor, cuando en la soledumbre
de algún quehacer o, a veces,
en el desasimiento así de extremo
recuentas los vacíos
detrás de ti; cuando pervives, poco,
lo todo aquello que no fue ni, acaso,
más que emplazado fin, sobrevivida
muerte inicial.
        Y entonces. Es entonces:
cuando te tumbas ¿ya? en tu ajada hamaca
de madurez.
        Te reconoces, mimo,
ejerciendo la nada que tu sabes
ser, el papel, la farsa;
te ves representar, valen espejos,
el personaje tú; te ves haciendo
de ti—¿recuerdas? niños:
"yo hago de rey" "yo no, yo de caballo"
"yo soy el mariscal" "pues yo, el mendigo"—
te ves montando, y todos, el tinglado
de cada cual farándula; pervives
tu representación y a cada ruido

Roadshow

When you feel you're in your—already?—retirable
maturity and you look back
over your shoulder at all the official
milestones, a meat hook
for pulling yourself up the wall,
afterward the kids, or maybe not, your plan
for putting by a little something for just in case,
and then the first gray hair
and you ask yourself
what's become of me? . . .
                Your gaunt reflection
stares back at you, enveloped
in such fear, when in the isolation
of some task, or sometimes
in a kind of extreme disinterest,
you take stock of the hollow spaces
behind you; when you relive, a little,
everything that's only been, perhaps,
leading you to nothing more than the end
of the first round of surviving death.
            And then. It's then:
when you flop down—already?—in the sagging hammock
of your maturity.
              You recognize yourself, mimic,
practicing the nothing you know yourself
to be, the roles, the farce: with the aid of mirrors
you see yourself representing
the character that's you, see yourself
playing yourself—remember? Children:
"I'll be the king." "Not me. I'm the horse."
"I'm the marshal." "Well, me, I'm the beggar."
You see yourself, and everyone, mounting the platform
knocked together for every such road show; you go on
with your act and at every sound

te vuelves pronto, saltas
temeroso, te afirmas,
—más para ti: los otros te soportan—
te hundes en tu solio
teatral, en tu grandeza vestuaria,
en tu miradme, soy el juez, palpadme,
soy el jerarca, el síndico, el poeta.

Y es entonces: cuando de tanto verte
y no quererte ver en tu penuria
desnudez. Es entonces.
                                    Con ojos
y con uñas, proteges,
por todo el resto ya, con aspavientos,
defiendes cada letra
de tu papel, exiges a los otros
la réplica, te aferras a la trama
de la farsa para seguir no siendo
en tu inventada realidad.
                                    Acaso
porque no hay otro modo
más tan humano de supervivencia.

you look around, shuffle
nervously, affirm yourself
—mostly for yourself; the others support you—
you're submerged in your simulated
throne, your costumed splendor,
in your: *Look at me, I'm the judge; touch me,
I'm the high priest, the trustee, the poet.*

And it's then: when from so much seeing yourself
and not wanting to look anymore at your miserable
nakedness. It's then.
                    To the eyeballs,
with fingernails, you protect,
by now to the bitter end, panting,
you defend every letter
of the role, demand that others
play their parts, you cling to the plot
of the farce, in order to go on not sensing
the invented reality you're living.
                        Maybe
because there's no other way
so human for surviving.

Moho

Huele in algunas casas
a oscuridad acumulada, a moho
hereditario. Pasas
el dintel, las torcidas
jambas y huele, y es de pronto, y cruzas
por el zaguán y huele
como si cada muerto
aún familiar hubiese,
al irse, tan derecho, hubiese ido
dejando alguna cosa
caer marchita, o gotas
de lividez, o líquidos horrendos,
hubiese con su labio
cerúleo y su algodón
en la nariz, hubiese como ido
soplando en las paredes, impregnando
de muerte suya corporal baldosas
y peldaños y zócalos, y fuese
su olor como una mancha que te asalta
desde la externa claridad del aire.

Subes las escaleras
de algunas casas y te sale al paso
en el rellano el denso
olor a todo lo que un día
estuvo vivo allí, estuviste vivo
en otra alguna vez, y pende ahora,
desgaste y desmemoria, de retratos
orlados con muchachas
ajadas, de tiestos
desportillados, flecos de mantones
en la pared, al saloncito, el mármol
de la consola, pende
deshilachado en colchas

Mold

It smells in certain houses
of accumulated gloom, hereditary
mold. As you cross
the threshold, past the warped
doorjamb, it smells right away, and you move
through the vestibule and it smells
as if every corpse
still at home there, had
in leaving, straight as he was, had departed
letting drop something
withered, or a livid
ooze, a loathsome fluid;
had, with his lips
gone blue and his nose stuffed
with cotton, it's as if he'd gone out
breathing into the walls, impregnating
floor tiles and steps and baseboards
with his bodily death, and it's
that odor like a stain that leaps at you
right out of the clear air outside.

Walk up the stairs
in certain houses and as you reach
the landing out comes the dense odor
of everything that once
was alive there—that you've lived
in some time or other—and it hangs there now,
fustiness and fading memories, from garlanded
portraits of girls who've lost
their bloom, from chipped
crockery, fringed shawls draped
on the walls, in the little parlor, the marble
of the console; it hangs there
unraveling in crocheted

de ganchillo, en plumíferas almohadas,
alcobas y humedad, desportillado
aguamanil, jofaina rinconera.

No huele a tierra húmeda ni a estiércol
saludable y honrado—diluirse
para más vida y vuelta—no; no hay ciclo
que justifique la largueza. Huele
a ya no queda calle
que respirar, a broza
de bodonal; y miras el pasillo
apenumbrado y puertas
entornadas y huele
a se acabó, por esta y para siempre
vez se acabó, y el golpe es desde dentro.

No más. La vida aquí, en algunas casas
se encharcó, cuchitriles
de nonatas hazañas, y ahora huele
—te estás oliendo tú—como enranciada
y pasas, y te pide
su preterida libertad, oliendo
a lo que es, a nada
fermentada, a desprecio, a ya no queda
aquí ni para el gasto de ir muriendo.

bedspreads, bursting feather-ticks,
bedroom dampness, a cracked
pitcher on the corner washstand.

It doesn't smell of damp earth
or wholesome, honest manure—melting down
for new life to come back—no, there's no cycle
that justifies this fulsomeness. It smells
of *There's no room to breathe*
here, like the rotting stubble
of mud flats; and you look at the hall's
faded light and half-closed
doors and it smells
used up, for now and for all time
used up, and the deathblow is from inside.

No more. The life here, in certain houses,
has gone stagnant, pigeonholes crammed
with things left undone, and now it smells—
it's yourself you're smelling—like it's rancid
and as you move on it pleads
for its cutoff freedom, smelling
of what it's become, of emptiness
fermented, of depreciation, of the lack here now
of even the price of going out dead.

Destajo

Está la luz tan tuya,
hermano, tan madera
tu rictus, tu perfil contra una finca,
ajeno señorio, y el destajo,
y el peso sobre un mango
de azadón, y el ajuste, y un a cuánto
el marjal, y un lo tomas o lo dejas
luminoso y tristísimo, que nimba
tu boina capada, tus abarcas. . . .
Está tan ascua el día
contra un todo descaro de olivares
andaluces, y cava aquí, y destripa
los terrones, rescata
el alijar, escarba las paratas. . . .
Está tan cal, tan fusta en plena cara
el cortijo murado, hoy parece
que vienen, la jarana,
el braceo nervioso
del alazán del amo. Está tan pozo
la guitarra y tirarse
a la negrura, pena va, del cante. . . .

Porque de tarde, la amargura, agua
que te regó el hondón como esponjoso,
no sabes, pecho adentro,
va a parar al azarbe con los otros
sobrantes, todo tuyo, en los que mucho
a mucho te descuajas,
en los que poco a poco te desvives.

Bramuras entre dientes y usted manda;
nervio cereño tras los ojos bajos;

Task Work

Today's light is so yours,
Brother, that grin carved out
of wood, your silhouette against a hillside,
somebody else's land, and the task work,
the heaviness over the handle
of a hoe, and the bargaining: a *So much
for the whole job, so take it or leave it,*
luminous and agonizing, that haloes your old beret
that's lost its tassel, your shuffle shoes. . . .
It's such a glowing coal, this day,
against the whole insult of an Andalusian
olive grove and a *Dig here, and root out
these clods, shore up
the landslides, scrape the terraces clean.* . . .
It's so whitewash glare, such a whiplash across the face,
the walled estate, and today they must
be coming, the uproar, the nervous stamping
of the owner's sorrel. It's so wellhole,
the guitar, and throwing yourself
into the blackness—look out below,
pain's coming—of the song. . . .

Because sooner or later the bitterness, water
that soaked the spongy bottomland,
you don't even know it, deep in your heart,
will end up down the ditch with the other
runoff, all yours, everything that much
by much you're gutted by, everything
that little by little you're dying of.

Curses between your teeth and *As you wish, sir,*
a dogged will behind the lowered eyes,

la cansera apoyada en el balate
y un ahogo coyunda
que te anuda el desprecio y la garganta.

Está tan tuya, hermano, la desmaña
ajada con que pisas
la ortiga, el desespero
a golpe de almocafre; está tan tuya
la calidez morada
de la lejana serranía, el siempre
tironeo de la querencia, tierra
de antepasados, la raigal costumbre
de otear la desgracia. . . .

Un verde oscuro encima los bancales
y la campal grandeza, así de ajena,
misera, más no cabe, el retraimiento
de tu pana gastada y tu perdone.
La luz, lo sólo tuyo, hacina lomas
para mirar, lo sólo tuyo: el tardo
mirar campero y paso en esta ronda.
A ver si hay suerte y pueden
entrar en juego, tú no ya, los hijos
de los hijos, quién sabe, de tus hijos.

Tajo parejo y vuelta a la faena,
que en esto de esperar no hay quien nos moje
a los hombres del sur; a los que quedan.

exhaustion propped against the terrace bank
and a suffocating bondage
that knots scorn around your throat.

It's so yours, Brother, your careless
slouch, stumbling through
the nettles, hope running out
with every stroke of the short-hoe, so yours,
the shimmering purple heat
over the far peaks, and always
your love of the land tugging at you, land
of your forebears, the way it's rooted in you
to see nothing but misery. . . .

A deep green hangs over the terraces
and the vast countryside, none of it yours,
despises—how else could it be—the servility
of your worn-out corduroys, and your *Sorry.*
The light, all that's yours, piles up hills
for looking at, all that's yours: the torpid
countryman's stare and *I'll pass this hand.*
Maybe we'll have some luck, and they
can get into the game, not you anymore, but the children
of the children, who knows, maybe of your children.

The same work to finish, so get on with it,
since when it comes to hanging on, there's no one can lick us
men of the South, what's left of us.

Desguace

Te me deshaces en el beso, amiga.
A lo largo del beso
van arrando tu piel ¡qué de otro tiempo!
las arrugas.
                    Te amo.
                            Se licúan
tus pómulos; se sume,
se desdenta tu boca y yo te amo.
Te me disuelves en el beso, amiga,
te me desnaces, ay, bajo este cuerpo
que cubre tu erosión.
                        Te me destrenzas.

Tu lagunal mirada verdinegra
que otro estiaje requebraja y otro . . .
dime si aún me ves . . .
                            tu voz gimiendo
que un zumbido o recuerdo lobreguece . . .
tu saética lengua acribarante . . .
la sed ya no precede . . .
                            tu cabeza
por mi hombro, tu redondez, tu espacio
antes tempero, tanto
todo y demás que queda en, mira,
un casi sequestal, sino esa lágrima
rezumada de zubias interiores. . . .

Un hasta luego ¿cuándo? en cada instante
que enmohece el latido; una maraña
de destejidos roces; un tan otro
aquel impulso y ¿cuánto es lo que queda?
un reloj que quebraza
los muros del deseo, que corroe
la dádiva, que enrancia los agraces;
un humedal que empapa los desechos.

Splintering

You're disappearing in this kiss, my friend.
Down the length of a kiss
time plows your skin—ah, but time that was—
with its furrows.
                    I love you.
                                    Silt. Bone, tooth,
cheek, melting away, caving in, and I love you.
This kiss can't hold you back, my friend,
from dissolving into your elements,
ay, beneath this body
that covers your erosion.
                            Hair abandoning its roots.

Your liquid darkgreen gaze a parched lagoon
checked by another drought and another . . .
tell me if you still see me . . .
                                    your voice querulous
as some dark chord or memory assails you . . .
the bitter darting tongue
thirsty for any moisture . . .
                                    your head
on my shoulder, your fullness, such amplitude
you spread out to be sown, such all
and everything and more, become—look, now—
an almost arid wasteland except for this teardrop
sprung from an underground stream. . . .

A good-bye—how soon?—in every moment
that molders the heartbeat; a tangle
of shared flesh, unraveling; such an otherness
that impulse now, and how much is left?
A clock that cracks the walls
of desire, that corrodes
the body's gift, sours the green wine;
a damp that soaks into the ruins.

Te me deshojas dentro del abrazo.
Te me lenteces bajo el pulso, amiga,
¿por qué no madre ya, de tan cobijo?
¿por qué no hermana en tanto
trasvase sangre a sangre?

                    Te me amainas,
te me remansas en el beso. Cuerpo
de grutas y de espuma, rocas húmedas
que la marea abandonó, ensenadas
con naufragios y mástiles
retorcidos y quillas
donde la herrumbre pone sus huevos amarillos. . . .
Tu prestancia abatida, tu tronchada
blancura cervical, tus senos cántaro
¡tan rotundo el ayer! altivos trojes
de caricias aquellas
que se enconaron, ay, tu quiebro airoso,
tu macerado vientre, así fecundo,
decadente añojal hasta el menguado
alcacel de tu vello.

Te me deslizas a la muerte.

                    Palpo
tus lugares vacíos, tus siniestras
oquedades, la nada
en donde estuvo tu hermosura.

                    Te amo.
Cobertizo que el tiempo zarandea.
Almáciga que asola la riada.
Roqueda que el verdín melancoliza.

Te me desguazas en el beso, amiga;
a lo largo del beso te me pierdes,
te me deslíes, ay, te me regresas
a la tierra, que absorbe,
que recupera así su amargo zumo.

Another leaf shed in this embrace,
a shifting ground beneath the pulse, my friend.
—Why not mother by now, after such nurturing?
Why not sister, from such a flowing
each into the other, blood to blood?
                                        Your great sails furled,
you're drifting shoreward down this kiss. Body
of spume and grottos, moist rocks
the tide abandoned, cove
of foundered ships, masts
twisted, upended keels
where the rust lays its yellow eggs.
Your ravaged elegance, the firm white column
of your throat, crumbling now, your breasts like vessels
—how filled to overflowing yesterday!—twin silos
rising proudly to the caresses
that swelled them, ah, your airy motions,
your leached-out belly, so fecund,
gone fallow now, sprouting only
a scanty ryegrass cover.

You're slipping away from me, down to death.
                              I grope
inside your empty places,
your woeful hollows, the nothing
where your beauty was.
                              I love you.
Wayside shelter rattled by gusts of time.
Seedbed swept away in the rising flood.
Sea rock saddened by the creeping green.

I feel you splintering in this kiss, my friend.
Down the length of a kiss I'm losing you
to your dissolution—ay, you're seeping back
into the earth that absorbs,
that repossesses thus its bitter juice.

Estancia

Cuando se fue, cuando el esparto alfombra
recuperó el espacio desplazado
por su peso y el aire
volvió a su sitio y la trenzada anea
de las sillas y el barro
de las baldosas y el encima y humo
del testero sobre el hogar volvían
a sentir el silencio lentamente
posándose y el frío;
cuando sonó la puerta
de cuarterones y, desde los zócalos
hasta las altas vigas y el crujente
cielo de la alfajía, el blancor todo
de la casa se fue como achicando,
la cal como apagando
su reverbero, y desde las barandas
del mirador lo afuera se veía
más solo aún y el miedo de volverse
y los pasillos en penumbra;

               cuando
el entreabrir los párpados y el manso
entrellorar, ya para qué, y el lastre
de otra forma de soledad y el pienso
que así está bien y el dejo
y la desmaña en colocar, en cada
rincón, embrazaduras
para el recuerdo y todo
como empezando a ser desde una externa
dimensión del asombro
no profanada por la ausencia;

               cuando
citaras y tabiques, aquí al lado
estaba, y encalada
tronera, persistía en su sedante

The Front Room

When it was gone, when a mat of rough grass
filled in the space its bulk
had taken up and the air
returned to its region and the plaited rush
of the chairs and the clay
of the firebrick, the cap and smoke
of the chimneypiece over the hearth began
to feel the silence slowly
settling in, and the cold;
when the great carved door banged
to and fro and, from baseboards
to high rafters and the creaking
boards of the ceiling, the whole brightness
of the house faded as though shrinking,
as if the light reflected by the whitewash
had gone out, and from the railings
of the lookout the grounds appeared
more isolated yet, the fear of coming back
and the darkening hallways;
                              when
with half-closed eyelids, the subdued
moment before tears—by now for what—and another
kind of solitude for ballast, the thought
that it's all right that way, the clumsy
trying to let go and finding,
in every corner, handholds
for memories and everything
beginning to seem from an outer
dimension of awesomeness,
not profaned by absence;
                              when
but bare walls and partitions, here it was
to one side, and plastered
porthole windows, persisting in its grave

no decir, y postigos y fallebas,
miraba amaitinando rachas, nubes,
aquí de asiento, y el cojín y el arco
y los herrajes, iba,
se movía en la sombra y mantenía
su ser en más allá de estas paredes,
de mis brazos, y andaba
como empezando a irse nunca;
                              cuando
ya traspasado el huerto, la cancela
chirriante, más lejos, se detuvo
en los primeros chopos del ribazo,
casi un momento, el tiempo
de arrancar una hilacha
de pasado y se hundió con el postrero
inútil aleteo de la tarde
derribada sobre el alero,
                              entonces,
tan sólo entonces, algo
ajeno y suyo y dentro y por encima
de la presencia, todo
lo que fue su presencia, desligado
de decadencia corporal, sin trabas
de entendimiento, algo
total, pura inmanencia, como vuelto
del otro lado ya de los sentidos,
fue invadiendo la estancia, fue tomando
posesión, llanto a llanto, del vacío,
se fue como quedando en lo que era
la única verdad, ya superados
los posibles, se fue como instalando
en la nada de ser, de haber no sido,
y al fin y para siempre.

not-speaking, and shutters and latches,
it watched scrutinizing gusts of wind, clouds,
sitting here, and the cushion, the chest,
the ironwork, it went on,
moved in the shadows and maintained
its being beyond these walls,
beyond my arms, and kept on
as if beginning never to go away;
                              when
now across the garden, the gate
creaking, beyond, it paused
among the first poplars on the rise
almost a moment, the time
it takes to grasp a strand
of the past, and sank with the last
useless wingflap of afternoon
spilling over the roofedge;
                        then,
and only then, something
other and its own and within and above
presence, everything
that was its presence, unleashed
from corporeal dissolution, not linked
to understanding, something
entire, pure immanence, returning as if
from the other side of the senses,
came invading that space, came taking
possession, groan by groan, of the emptiness,
came as though fixed in whatever was
the only truth, all possibilities
already disposed of, came as if giving itself
to unbecoming, to never having been,
and finally and forever.

About the Author

Rafael Guillén was born in Granada, Spain, in 1933 and still calls the city his home. His many books of poetry include *La configuración de lo perdido: Antología, 1957–1995*, *Versos del amor cumplido: Antología 1956–1985*, and *Los estados transparentes*. He is a major "Fifties Generation" poet, and his work has been widely translated. In 1994 he was awarded Spain's National Prize for Literature for *Los estados transparentes* after having been a finalist for the Critics' Prize.